How to Make Money
Get Off Your Ass & Make Some Cash
by Dawn Xhudo

How to Make Money

Get Off Your Ass & Make Some Cash

By Dawn Xhudo

Copyright Dawn Xhudo 2012

Dedication

I want to dedicate this book to my husband, Tony who is and always be the light of my life which really did not begin until the day we met. He is the true one and only love of my life. I love you Jerk!

TABLE OF CONTENTS

<u>Chapter 1</u>
USE POSITIVE THINKING TO GET WHAT YOU WANT

It really surprises me when people wake up broke, know that they are broke and don't know how they are going to go about making money for what they need. Even if it is a couple dollars to get themselves thru the day. There is an entire world of possibilities out there and all you have to do is go out and get what you need. I don't mean to hit a little old lady over the head and steal her social security check I mean there is a lot of potential and I will help you find the many different ways that you can make money when you really need it.

The first thing they think is "Oh shit I'm broke!" the next thought is "Where am I going to get money?" With those thoughts in mind they don't have a clue as to where to go about getting money because the next thought is "Who can I borrow money from?" This is the wrong direction to go in because you're going to have to pay that money back at some point and if you borrow from some shady character your might end up with your legs broken!

So the first thing you want to do when you wake up broke and ask yourself those questions you should change the last question to "How can I make some money?". Making your own money will make you feel much better about yourself knowing you are not depending on someone else to make it.

I will give you the ideas and all you have to do is run with them. Take them as they are or put your own twist on them. Make them your own. Hopefully by the time you are done reading this you will have the ability to make something out of nothing and have money in your pocket. There are ways to make money all around you.

What it all boils down to is you need to change the way you think. If your lazy and don't want to help yourself then this book is not for you and you will not make money. You will probably quit and then go borrow money from someone. Then you will stay on the same lazy broke path you have been on forever.

But if you are the type of person who legitimately does not know how to the make money that is all around you then you have the potential to open that way of thinking up. We all have potential, we all have a special skill something that you were born with, something that comes naturally to you. Not everybody is able to do what comes naturally to you so you have the ability to use that skill and make money selling it to those of us who were not born with your special skill. There is a market out there for everything. In other words there is someone out there to purchase any thing that you have to market. Why do you think ebay is so successful? There are people out there selling rocks, snips of hair, etc... One guy sold a piece of toast because he said it had come out of the toaster and there was a picture of the Virgin Mary on it. I bet you can search for the stupidest thing you can think of and it will be for sale on ebay. I know I used to sell on ebay and I have put things on there that you would not think would sell and I sold it! No shit! I sold it and it went for a lot more than I thought that it was worth!

Did you ever hear the saying? "One man's trash is another man's treasure? Well that is what I am talking about here. I will show you how to make the money that you need in simple to follow steps. All you have to do is be positive and it will work out for you.

<u>Chapter 2</u>
A GREAT & FUN WAIT TO MAKE MONEY

In this chapter I will start giving you some ideas of how to make money out of what seems like your starting with nothing. Believe me there have been more days than I wish to admit that I woke up broke. More people than not wake up broke. We are the majority and it can be overwhelming, discouraging, and down right degrading to wake up broke. The feelings of desperation take over, you have to admit that the thought of robbing a bank has entered your mind, fantasizing about what it would be like. But then your rational takes over and you know that your not going to rob a bank even though you would like to! My point here is don't let it get you down. Your not going to take it anymore and you are going to make money. Get it in your head! Focus on it and be positive. It will come to you. It is all in the power of positive thinking. If you want it, say it, think it, and know your going to get it. I can not tell you how many times in my life that there were things that I wanted. Did I get everything I ever wanted? Not really, I wish I could say that I have but I can't and I will not tell you that you will get everything you want either. But you can't sit on your couch and expect it to come and knock on your door because that is not going to happen. What you need to do is use positive thoughts that clear your head, look for any step that can you can take to get you closer to your goal and take it. Negativity, procrastination, and fear will not get you there. These are all negative things.
It all boils down to you can get what you want if you get the negative out of your mind and life. Negative thoughts cloud your thinking and bring negative things to you. Positive thinking clears you mind so you can think clearly, see opportunity so you can take action to get you closer to your goal!

If you are in need of fast cash like I said earlier most people's first thought would be who can I borrow money from. We are not going to even discuss this because you are not going to do that.

I am a self proclaimed "hustler" not meaning that I hustle people for money. I mean that I hustle to get what I want. I have initiative and drive. I will tell you some of the things that I have done to make money without a job.

My favorite way to make money without a job is to go on Craiglist. I will go one there and look through the free items. There is always something good on there. People that are moving always give away good items. I will contact them, go pick it up, take pictures of it and re-post it for sale! You can even check out the wanted section on craigslist there may be someone looking for what you have just acquired. I have never been stuck with something that I could not sell! This is a great system and it will cost you nothing but time! Usually depending on how good the item is you can probably sell it the same day and there you go you have cash in a day!

I have sold everything from clothes to refrigerators that I got for free on Craigslist!

Another way to make money is to post your own ad on Craigslist that you would like yard sale leftovers, garage and attic items that are not wanted anymore. But you need to specify that you are not a garbage man and that you would like only items that can be reused. There you go you now have a ton of free stuff that you can post and sell. If you have a garage you can put a Yard Sale sign at the end of your drive way and have a Yard Sale every weekend. You can sell the free stuff that you obtained thru your ad and make more money. This is something that I have done. I acquired antiques, furniture, clothes, you name it and made a ton of money on the weekends. I literally would have people knocking on my door when I was not having a sale looking to buy stuff that they had seen at my sale or they were looking for a specific item and wanted to know if I had it. So I had money knocking on my door!

Chapter 3
MAKE THE MOST PROFIT

My next favorite way to make money is to sell old books. Now you don't have to sell old books because I do. You can sell any kind of book you wish to sell. I just happen to have a niche for old books. The most cost effect way to get books to sell is to find out if your local library has a bookstore. They sell all of the books that they take out of their inventory and people donate books to them as well. They usually sell paperbacks for $.50 and hardcovers for $1.00. This leaves it open for a large profit margin if when you sell them. If you get something really good you will make a lot of money on them. I have found autographed books at the library book store! If you can get in good with the people who run the bookstore they will let you pick out of the books that have been donated before they go on the shelf for sale. This will give you the chance to get the really good stuff. If they really like you and you buy a lot of books they may also give you a discount. Leaving some of the books at 100 percent profit when you sell them!

Another good way of getting books is going to yard sales. If you don't see books always ask if they have them. I once went to a yard sale and asked I ended up in a dusty attic. I got 4 boxes of books for $10.00. In those boxes there was one book that I ended up selling on ebay for

$600.00. It was an autographed copy of the The Last Weekend. Always ask if you don't see any!

You can also put an ad on craigslist asking for books. You may get more responses than you care to pick up.

Now that you have the books where are you going to sell them. Well you can start an ebay seller's account, amazon.com seller account, abebooks.com, biblio.com just to mention a few online sites that let you set up accounts to sell your inventory. You can even put them on craigslist but the other book selling sites are much more effective.

Get to know books, authors, publishers this will give you an advantage when you are purchasing books. You will know their worth. If you have an ipad or kindle you can also take this with you to the bookstore giving you a chance to look the book up and see what it is worth before you purchase it.

I have made a lot of money selling books online. I have sold everything you can think of online. Books have the largest profit margin. They are easy to ship most of the time you can just bubble wrap them and slip them into a manila envelope. If you are shipping a rare book I recommend bubble wrap and a book box. The shipping on books is also very low because of media mail. This keeps your overhead at a minimum.

I also would advise if you are going to sell books to get a book on books & rare books. This will tell you what books are sought after, what publisher's, illustrators, markings, etc... to look for as well as giving you a sample of the author's signature. Anyone can pick up a sharpie and sign a book. Be very careful when dealing with autographed books. Get to know how to tell a first edition because not all first editions state that they are especially the older ones. The more modern books might state that they are first editions. Check the verso (this is the flip side of the title page) this usually will tell you the edition of the book.

Take pictures of the books and when you are describing them in your ad be sure to notate any damage to the book even shelf wear. This will save a lot of trouble later with returns. You can even take pictures of the damage so anyone interested in the book is well aware before they make the purchase. Always be honest! It does not pay in the long run to hide imperfections the person buying the book will see it when it is delivered to them any way. This may cause you to have to refund their money and pay extra shipping charges when you are making the refund.

<u>Chapter 4</u>
EATING YOUR WAY TO PROFIT

I guess by now you know where I am going with this. You can virtually find money anywhere as long as you have the initiative to do so. Like I said earlier if your lazy and expect money to come knocking on your door while you watch a movie or play x-box than you will more than likely be broke for a while to come.

Now on to more ways of generating cash flow. A good way to make money if you like to cook is to offer catering services to friends and family. If you feel really ambitious you can always place an ad offering your services to the public. Just don't bite off more than you can chew at first. I know sometimes offers can arise that are very tempting because of the money that is being offered but you have to be realistic. If you accept the job, take the money and it is more than you can handle it will fall apart. This will cause you all kinds of problems including having to pay back all of that money. This is what we want to avoid. So keep a level head and know what you can handle.

If you really are a "foody" You love to eat and you love to cook you could offer cooking lessons to the less fortunate that do not know how to cook! You can do something you love and make money at it! You can post fliersand do private lessons or find a place where you conduct a full blown class on cooking. You could even break it down to dinners, breakfasts, deserts, etc... offer a class on each one.

If you like to bake do a flier for wedding cakes, birthday cakes, cupcakes, etc. You could bake a bunch of samples of your work and hand them out with a business card or flyer at your local grocery store or mall. Just check with the mall or store first to get the okay to be there. You don't want to go out and not get permission first and then get arrested with your wares in tow. This would just cost you money!

If you don't know how to cook or are an amateur but would love to cook for a living. Get your cookbook out and learn! Find out what you cook the best and specialize in it. There is a market for almost anything out there. Learn your craft. Even professionals are learning something new every day. There is no way that anyone can be the leading authority on something and know absolutely everything there is to know about anyone subject. Work for your dream. There are thousands upon thousands of rags to riches stories out there of people who started their businesses with twenty dollars or less. You just have to be motivated to do so. So put your big boy or girl pants on and let's get to work. Like I said before and will keep drilling this into your head....It is not going to come knocking on your door!

CHAPTER 5

GROWING YOUR PROFIT

My next suggestion for making money would be to advertise your skill for yard work and gardening if you love plants and gardening. You could offer to do anything from trimming hedges to maintaining gardens. You can mow, edge, prune, trim, plant, water, etc. a lot of people do not like to do these things and find them utterly mundane. That's the ticket to making money on things like this. A lot of people do not like to do them and do not want to make the time to do it. The good thing about this kind of work is you can tell by driving past who your potential customers may be. You can target them by putting one of your fliers in a plastic hang bag and hang it off the handle of the mailbox! DO NOT EVER PUT ANYTHING INSIDE A MAILBOX! I can not stress that enough because if you do you may be opening yourself up to tampering with someone's mail which is a federal offense. If you want to be really ambitious you can go door to door and present your flier. This is a bit more direct and you can have a chance to win over your potential customer. You can even offer to do extras such as drive way sealing, gutter cleaning, taking out the trash, shoveling snow in the winter time, cleaning the yard, attic, or garage. Only if you have experience cutting down trees do you offer this service. There are a hoard of dangers both to yourself, someone else or a financial danger if the tree falls on something or someone. So please do not offer to do this unless you have done it before. The same goes for really high gutter cleaning. If you are not experienced in doing this or roof work I would not advise that you offer to do this.

You should also check with the management offices for housing communities in your area. A lot of these places either violate or fine residents that do not mow their grass. You can explain what you do and ask them if it is okay to post some of your fliers for your services.

There are a few things that you may need to own to do this like a lawnmower, shovels, rakes, edger, weed whacker, etc. But there is also the possibility that the people that you are working for may also have these and may let you use them to complete the task. It would be better if you had your own tools just in case you get the job and they do not have their own. What do you do then?

You also may want to read a few books on plants and trees if you plan on pruning, etc... just so you know what time of the year you should be doing this. You do not want to kill someone expensive trees, plants or bushes if you prune them the wrong time of the year. You can also look up a few agricultural websites to get this info. Also use the Farmer's Almanac it can be very useful. The website is:
http://www.farmersalmanac.com/weather/2011/08/29/2012-us-winter-forecast/

CHAPTER 6
CASHING IN THE BLING

There are times when we all find ourselves broke in between paychecks wondering how the heck we will make it until the next payday. Where will you find the money? Well this one is a simple no brainer. You can look around and see what you have in your house that you no longer want or are not using. The fastest way to make money is to look around your home for items that you no longer need or want.

If you have jewelry and want to sell it be very careful and do not sell it to the first person that gives you an offer. Get a couple offers or have your item appraised by someone who is not going to be purchasing your item. The reason I say this is obvious, they may low ball the price just so they can save themselves some money. If you only need a few bucks to get you thru the day and do not want to sell the item you can just pawn the item and then get it back when you have the money. It is like selling it with out selling it and you do not have to pawn it for the entire value. You can pawn it for what ever amount you need. This will make it easier for you to get it back later.

Clean out the attic, garage or storage room. I am sure you will find things that you have forgotten about and have not seen in years. If you have not seen them in years or have not used them I am sure that you do not need them. Why not turn them into something that you do need like money!

Be very careful with any item that may have exceptional value such as jewelry, antiques, rare books, etc... Not everyone is honest and may like I said low ball you to try and buy and save themselves some money. The very same money that you can use.

Like I mentioned earlier you can have a yard sale, put an ad on craigslist, sell it on ebay or pawn it! This will give you enough cash to get thru to your next payday.

CHAPTER 7
WALK OR SIT YOUR WAY TO RICHES

If you have a love for pets, taking care of animals and can't get enough of going to the zoo or shelter than this next tip may just be the thing you need to make some dough.

You can advertise pet sitting or dog walking and walk your way to money. Animal kennels charge up to $100 a day to keep your pet while you are on vacation. This may work to your advantage since the pet owners will not only save themselves money but their beloved pets can stay right in the safety of their own home. All you have to do is make visits there to feed, water and walk. Of course if you are a true lover of pets you will take some time to cuddle, pet and play with them as well.

The best part is that you can do this for more than one family at a time since the pets are staying in their own homes. All you have to do is go from home to home.

You may also be able to offer house sitting services as well. In this day and age no one can ever be too sure of what they are going to come home to when they come back from an extended vacation. You can offer them that peace of mind. You will offer to check on the place, bring in news papers and mail so that it looks like someone is home. You might want to turn on a different light each day or leave a tv on so it looks like someone has been there. This also save the vacationer time because they do not have to call and put newspaper services on hold or have the post office put a hold on their mail while they are away.
With all of this in mind you may be able to make some extra cash by mowing the grass, watering the plants, weeding the garden, washing the cars, etc... The possibilities are endless. Use your imagination and you will make money.

CHAPTER 8
GOT ANY CASH HANDY?

As I mentioned in the earlier chapter for lawn care you could just drive around and see your potential customers. In this chapter we will talk about house care. If you just drive around you can spot the number of homes that are in disrepair. They need painting, roofing, siding, gutters, concrete work, etc.

Under the same principal you could offer these services for a fee. You can do a flier and put it on the mailbox (never inside) or you could use initiative and knock on the door, introduce yourself, and sell your services. Always be sure to look your best while you are doing this. You do not want to knock on the door in disarray. Be sure to have your hair combed, have on clean clothes, and you look your best. When you look your best, you feel your best, and you can sell your best. If they are vacant homes you can go on the tax roll website for that town or county, look up the address and this will tell you who the current owner is. In light of the current foreclosure situation in this company it just may be a bank. You can contact the bank and see if they are interested in your services to keep vandals away from the house. You just may end up with all of their houses to tend to! This also works well with real estate firms that have a bunch of foreclosed homes to get rid of. You never know some of these jobs could turn into bigger and better things for you. If the homeowner owns more than one home you could possibly get a job taking care of any homes that they have. Again please do not offer services that you do not know how to do or can not perform. In the end it will make you look bad to the customer and they will not offer you any more work. Please be sure to check your local and state laws before embarking on any work. There may be licenses or permits needed for certain work.

CHAPTER 9
JACK OF ALL TRADES

In this day there are too many elderly people out there with no care givers. On any given day you can turn on the news and hear about the old man that wandered off and could not find his way back home. The elderly lady who was mugged in an elevator or was found in her filthy home eating cat food because she could not get out to buy real food. With that said there is a large market for people to either sit with the elderly or take them shopping. You could run errands to the store, take them to the doctors or pharmacy. Once you hook up with one elderly person they tell their friends so a lot of your business will be word of mouth. Before you know it you will need a second person to help with all of the things that they need done, This is especially so if you get work in a senior housing development.

They may just want you to take a walk or sit with them. You could get work cleaning their homes, washing their cars (they can no longer drive). Walk their pets. The possibilities are endless. What it boils down to is they have no one to care for them and most of their kids more than likely live far away with families of their own.

This one may entail a little of all of the other job suggestions. They could need repairs done to their homes or cars. Most of the elderly population do not trust anyone coming in to their homes so you may have to earn their trust. Once you get in the door they will tell their friends about you this may lead to more calls for work!

You may find yourself watering their plants, cutting their grass, walking their dogs, painting their homes. Grocery shopping, picking up their medication at the pharmacy, taking them to the doctors, yard work, and taking them to cash their social security checks.

One thing is for sure you will never stop hearing stories of when they worked, went to war, their younger years, how they met, what achievements their kids have made and when the last time they went to bathroom was!

CHAPTER 10
PICTURE THIS

A fun way to make some cash with minimal effort is to take pictures of anything that you can think of. Take pictures of people doing anything you can think of or any kind of animal that you can catch on film. Be sure to get permission if you are taking pictures of people. You can then take those photos and download them. Once you get them downloaded you can start your own website to sell stock photos. There is a great demand for these photos for websites, e-books, regular books, fliers, businesses, etc...

People are willing to pay big bucks for the royalty free photos. This is a fun and great way to earn some cash. You may want to set up a paypal account so you can accept credit card payments on your website if you don't already have one.

While I am on the subject another great way to make money is to write your own e-books. People are always willing to pay for information. You can sell articles on certain subjects or you can sell entire e-books. You will have to know how to market the e-books
so you might want to research this before you start your writing career. There is a great demand for e-books.

You can research what the best sellers are before you start to give yourself an idea of what people are looking for. You might even be a great writer and want to write your first novel to sell. I can tell you that romance novels sell like crazy so if you want to go this route it will not do you wrong!

You could also blog. There are a lot of websites out there that will pay you to write articles for them. There are websites that will pay you to do surveys. Google adsense will pay you by click to place their ads on your blog or website and you get paid each time someone clicks on the ad!

You could also become an affiliate to almost any website out there. Place their ads on your site or blog and you get paid when someone either buys something or clicks on the ad.

You can become a freelance writer and offer your services. You can find ads from websites looking for freelance writers.

CHAPTER 11
BEING A SMART ASS CAN PAY OFF!

Did you do good in school? Are you an authority on a certain subject? Do you have a bunch of useless information that you have never needed trapped in your head? If so you can place ads to tutor or teach someone what you know.

Offer classes on the subjects or you can offer hour classes to kids who are getting ready to take a test or need to pass a certain subject in school.

You can also teach classes on what ever subject you are the master of. If you are an extremely good painter you can offer painting classes. If you are a great baker then teach a baking or cooking class. Do you see where I am going with this?

Again use your imagination to create the class you feel most comfortable that you know enough about to teach.

Put up fliers for tutoring or for the class that you want to have. State what the cost will be and request that people email you to register for the class. This way you know how many to expect. Also you can check with your local VFW or anywhere they may have a room that you can use for this class.

Be sure you have all of the materials that you will use for the class ready before that date. Also do your research because you do not want to get up in front of a room of people and not know what you are talking about.

CHAPTER 12
A FEW MORE WAYS TO MAKE CASH

Your opinion really does count so why not make some money giving it. You can take online surveys to make some extra money. Just don't ever pay anyone to give you a job. There are a lot of scam artist out there today so if anyone asks you to give them money to give you a job tell them no thanks and move on.

There are a lot of businesses out there that will pay for your opinion. You can check out the nearest companies to you that will pay you to be part of a focus group. All you have to so is sit in a room with other people and talk about what you think on a certain subject or product.

If you are looking for a work at home job I am going to say it again.....DON'T EVER PAY ANYONE TO GIVE YOU A JOB!!!! You can find hundreds of companies that are looking to hire people to work at home. It works out great for the companies because they do not have to pay the overhead to have on site employees. Most of the jobs are for independent contractors so they do not have to pay over time, vacation pay, sick pay, etc...If you would like more info on this subject you can check out my other book Legitimate Work at Home Jobs & Where to Find Them at : http://www.amazon.com/Legitimate-Work-Home-Where-

ebook/dp/B008GUMHHA/ref=sr_1_3?
ie=UTF8&qid=1347774503&sr=8-3&keywords=xhudo

It lists over 100 legitimate companies that are looking to hire people to work at home!

You can donate blood or spem for cash. You can sell your eggs and there are people that will also buy your hair to make wigs. Like I said earlier there is a market for just about anything. There are people selling pieces of toast and rocks on ebay for heaven's sake so if you have a service or a product there is a market out there for it. Don't ever let that last question be "Who can I borrow money from. Have some initiative and make some money on your own. Be inidependent go out and get what you want in life and never ask anyone for anything again.

For any questions that you may have or if you would just like to pick my brain you can contact me at: dawn.xhudo@yahoo.com

Please be sure to put the title of the book in the subject line so you are not skipped over!

Thank you for purchasing my book I do hope that it helped you out!

Tired of the BS Work at Home Scams?

I am too! That's why I have written this no nonsense guide to Legitimate Work at Home Jobs and Where to Find Them. I have included over 100 companies that are looking for people to work from home.

They Include jobs in a lot of different fields. There will be no stuffing envelopes, no making bead bracelets, and definitely no scamming of other people to earn back the money that you wasted on some scam website that promised to make you rich!

You will find tips on interviewing & what to put on your resume. Tips on how to get thru the interview and what to expect from the companies that are looking for people to work at home.

Please stay away from all of those get rich scams. Read this book and you will never be taken by one of these scam artists again!

Barcode Area

We will add the barcode for you.

Made with Cover Creator

LEGITIMATE WORK AT HOME JOBS & WHERE TO FIND THEM

Dawn Xhudo

Available in e-book or paperback

www.ingramcontent.com/pod-product-compliance
Lightning Source LLC
Chambersburg PA
CBHW041319180526
45172CB00004B/1160